GENOCIDE
IN
SRI LANKA

GENOCIDE IN SRI LANKA

M. S. VENKATACHALAM

Forewords by

M. Sivasithamparam, ***President, TULF***
A. Amirthalingam, ***Sect. General, TULF***

GYAN

ISBN : 978-81-212-0098-1

Published, 2018

Published by

Gyan Publishing House
5, Ansari Road
Daryaganj, New Delhi-110002
Phone: 011-47034999, 9811692060
www.gyanbooks.com
E-mail: books@gyanbooks.com

Printed at: G. Print Process, Delhi.

M. SIVASITHAMPARAM'S FOREWORD

IN recent times, to fight for freedom by the Tamils of Eelam in Sri Lanka has attracted the attention of many nations. The horrors of genocide perpetrated on the Tamils have pained and angered all freedom-loving peoples. They have demonstrated their intense resentment in different ways.

Mr. Venkatachalam has chosen to tell the world our righteous cause in this booklet. Mr. Venkatachalam is ideally suited to write on this subject. He has been associated with D.M.K. for many years and during these years he has been specially interested in the problems of Ceylon Tamils. He has made a study of our problems and he has set them down in this booklet with fervour born out of his love for Tamil and Tamils.

I thank him for his continued dedication to our cause.

President
Tamil United Liberation Front

M. SIVASITHAMPARAM

A. AMIRTHALINGAM'S FOREWORD

THE family of Sri Lanka have become one of the most oppressed nations of the world. The gory details of the torture, killings and genocide inflicted on them in the months of June, July and August 1983 have horrified the whole world.

Mr. M.S. Venkatachalam, M.A., B.L., advocate, a veteran in politics and Journalism has brought out the background to these incidents and a mass of testimony by eye-witnesses to them in this well written booklet. The thanks of the Eelam Tamils are due to Mr. Venkatachalam for his efforts in this regard. I am confident this book will enable all friend of the Tamils to understand their case better.

Secretary General A. AMIRTHALINGAM
Tamil United Liberation Front
Moolai-Chulipuram
Sri Lanka

CONTENTS

1

CINDRELLAS IN SRI LANKA

EVER since the British left the shores of Sri Lanka (then known as Ceylon), the island has witnessed numerous dastardly outbursts—the minority Tamils had been invariably the target of attack.

The island breathed air of freedom—but the Tamils were slowly but steadily subjugated by the Sinhalese and they were made second class citizens !

The Sinhalese leaders vied with one another in beating war-drums and singing war hymns against the Tamils !

Every one of them without exception preached 'moderation', 'compassion', 'parity' and the like, professed to be sympathetic towards Tamils and immediately after ascending the gadi, revealed his or her true colour and fell in line with Sinhalese fanatics !

The late lamented Chief Minister of Tamil Nadu and the beloved leader of all Tamils, *Mr. Anna,* with his own characteristic style and foresight wrote during 1958, "*whichever party attempts to control the Ceylon Government, must necessarily pander to the tastes of the mass of Sinhalese who are being tutored by fanatics. So each party in Ceylon has to compete with the other to prove that it is more Sinhalese than all other parties. In this race for supremacy the various political parties in Ceylon are led to become more and more antagonistic to the Tamilian interests and aspirations.*

"*Tamilians in Ceylon have seen many a change in the political scenery, but find their lot getting worse day by day. One butcher is as savage as another, for everyone of them is out for our blood...*" ("Homeland", April 20, 1958). His prophecy has been clearly proved, by now !

CIVIL RIGHTS FORFEITED

Immediately after independence, the so-called national Government brought in a legislation Citizenship Act of 1948—depriving the Tamils of Indian origin, their civil rights !

These persons had toiled in the island for more than a century ! By their sweat and toil, they had converted moors into mansions !

These teaming millions—all Tamils—were responsible for the growth of tea as well as rubber plantations. By their strenuous and breath-taking labour, the island is now having about 4,00,000 acres of tea plantation and 6,00,000 acres of rubber plantation.

Tea and rubber form the backbone of Sri Lankan economy —more than 70% of the country's foreign exchange is earned from tea and rubber and so the Tamils have contributed a lot towards the building of its economy.

The experts on tea industry estimate that Sri Lanka's tea industry depends almost 75% on Tamils. They say, "With Tamils gone, Sri Lanka can forget tea and get out of the business altogether."

Of course the plantations were declared as national wealth,

but the Tamils who were responsible for such national wealth were deprived of their citizenship rights by one stroke and they were declared "Stateless persons".

This was the first step taken towards subjugating the Tamil population and it was followed by a number of other measures !

ONSLAUGHT ON THE LANGUAGE

1956 elections were heralded as a Sinhalese Buddhist resurgence and it proved to be true too !

Mr. Bandaranaika (SLFP) as well as UNP were committed till then to preserve Sinhala-Tamil parity !

But as soon as he got into power, Mr. Bandaranaika went back on his commitment. The characteristic Sinhalese trait of assuring and abrogating came to the fore and he passed a sinister legislation called *Sinahlese only Act* (1956). The much-adored and often committed parity theory was given an unceremonious go-bye !

Of course, there were protests—much furore in the parliament and outside—the Tamil leaders could see the sinister motive behind the move but of no avail !

The brute majority Banda was having did not heed to the voice of reason—nay, they were not prepared to budge even an inch !

Though a provision was made for the reasonable use of Tamil in limited areas and for limited purposes, this provision remained only a dead letter !

The fear expressed by Tamil leaders like Mr. Chelvanayagam became true and the Tamils were slowly made the second class citizens !

SYSTEMATIC DISCRIMINATION

Minority Rights Group, a London-based Human Rights

Association has published a report, which clearly brings out the fact that the Tamils have suffered a lot because of the systematic discriminations of successive Governments of Sri Lanka.

Quoting a Trade Union of Government servants, Arasanga Eluthu Vinaya Sangam, the report says that between 1956 and 1970, the percentage of Tamils in the elite service fell from 30 to 5—in the sphere of subordinate clerical service, the fall is from 50% to 5%—in teaching, technical medical streams the fall is from 60% to 10%—in the armed forces the strength of Tamils fell from 40% to 1% and in the lowest categories the fall was from 40% to 5%.

The Report further adds that there has been a steady move to keep the Tamils away from acquiring higher education. The *University of Ceylon* conducted a study of Ethnic Recruitment between 1970 and 1975. Findings are as follows :

Tamil Entrants	1970	1975
1. Engineering Course	40.8%	13.2%
2. Medicine	37%	20%

STANDARDISATION

Thus the Sinhalese have slowly and systematically eliminated the Tamils from all spheres ! For the purpose of eliminating the Tamils from the sphere of higher education, they introduced a sinister system called standardisation. No parity now ! Equality is eschewed ! According to this system, a Tamil student has to score more marks than his Sinhalese counterpart to secure the same seat !

This awful discrimination has created an indelible impression and unshakable apathy in the minds of Tamil students and youth against the Sinhalese !

So, the successive Governments in their bid to capture the minds of the Sinhalese fanatics, have created a wide chasm between the two races and only the Sinhalese are to be blamed for sowing such a dragon's teeth !

The Ceylon Institute of National and Tamil Affairs submitted a Memorandum to the International Commission of Jurists. In its memorandum it has pointed out that a Tamil student has to secure 250 marks in the aggregate for securing a seat in the medical course, while his Sinhalese counter-part can secure the same seat with only 220 marks in the aggregate. Similar difference and discrimination exist as regards admissions to other science courses also, according to the submitted memorandum !

This atrocious scheme of standardisation was introduced and enforced under *Standardisation Act of 1970*. According to this Act, only persons learning Sinhalese upto X Std. are eligible for Government jobs, whereas Sinhalese need not study Tamil !

All these discriminatory acts of the successive Sinhalese Governments led to the formation of *Manavar Peravai* (Students' Federation) in 1972 in Jaffna. This Federation put forth its demand for a separate Tamil State !

Two years later, in 1974, *Ilaignar Peravai* (Youth Federation) consisting of students and youth was formed to fight for the cause of a separate Tamil State ! This Federation also pledged its faith in non-violence. From 1961 to 1972, the demand was only for a Federal status—then the Tamils, forced by Sinhalese fanaticism, are now on the verge of agitating for a separate state !

COLONISATION

Another factor which has made the Tamils of Sri Lanka a disgruntled group is the Government-sponsored colonisation !

AXE ON EMPLOYMENT

By shutting down the avenues of higher education, the Sinhala governments slowly deprived the employment opportunities of Tamils. The Tamil public servants who were already in employment were forced to study the Sinhalese language for

APPOINTMENT OF OFFICERS

Past 1977-1980	*Total appointments*	*Sinhalese*	*Tamils*	*% of Tamils who constitute 25.2% of the population*
Teachers	25,081	22,399	2,632	10.7%
Sri Lanka Administrative Service	144	144		
Translators	5	5		
Postmasters Signallers	46	44	2	4.5%
Government Service Clerks	3,326	3,127	199	5.9%
Typists	414	376	38	9.2%
Stenographers	198	135	63	31.8%
Book-keepers	183	172	11	6.1%
Railway Department Officers	195	181	14	7.2%
Railway Clerks	214	209	5	2.3%
Railway Guards	83	82	1	1.2%
Servants in the Govt. Secretariat at Tirumalai	20	16	4	15.0%
Pharmacists and Radiographers	480	473	7	1.4%
Persons selected by the Government for employment opportunities abroad in 1977-80	2,643	2,417	226	8.5%
Employees of the Prima Flour Mill permitted by the Ministry of Planning and Implementation	451	379	72	9.2%

(From Mr. M.V.M. Alagappan's "Tears in Teardrop Island")

retaining their jobs, getting increments and promotions. The racial discrimination against Tamils in employment can be seen from the statistics given below.

Those in service

Departmeut	*Total*	*Sinhalese*	*Tamils*	*% of Tamils*
Police	17,000	16,050	940	5.0%
Army	10,000	9,780	220	2.2%
Navy	2,170	2,084	146	6.7%

This was really a calculated onslaught on the economy of Tamils—really an economic strangulation. The dimension of the economic strangulation can be had from the statistics given on page 6.

Another factor which has made the Tamils of Sri Lanka a disgruntled group is the government-sponsored colonisation !

The Sinhalese were frequently dumped in the northern and eastern districts of Sri Lanka—the districts where the Tamils form an absolute majority.

This process of colonisation has been taking place ever since the independence of Sri Lanka, with a clear, but sinister motive of reducing the political strength of Tamils—this is a process of slowly annihilating and egging on the Tamils.

No amount of protest, not even furore, could stop this colonisation and the Tamils are very much perturbed by this !

Due to the colonisation, the Sinhalese population in Jaffna increased in three times between 1953 and 1971, while in the same period the Tamil populatian did not even double !

In Batticoloa (east Sri Lanka) the increase in Sinhalese population was thrice, while the Tamil population stood almost standstill.

In Triconamalee, there were not even 30 Sinhalese in 1898—but in 1982 they were more than 3 lakhs !

Therefore there has been a constant and calculated move to finish Tamils off, to deprive them of all their legitimate rights and to make them virtually a second-class citizens—the Cindrellas ! They can raise their voices and cry, weep and wail, but no place in positions of power. They can vote this or that Sinhalese leader to power, but they cannot demand, nor even expect those leaders to render justice ! The Sinhalese leadery will be going on and on in the beaten track of trampling the Tamils !

Put in such a precarious predicament, the Tamils have faced frequent and frenzied attacks of Sinhalese fanatics and the chasm between the two races have been increasing day by day, the Tamils completely losing faith in Sinhalese leaders, who have been adepts in the art of sabre-rattling, liberal in giving assurances, but lamentably vulgar in quickly abrogating them !

2

EVOLUTION OF EELAM MOVEMENT

THE multipronged suppression of successive Sri Lanka governments made Tamils lose their faith slowly in the theory of co-existence with the Sinhalese. It led to the formation of MANAVAR PERAVAI (Students' Federation) in 1972 in Jaffna. This Federation put forth its demand for a separate Tamil State !

Two years later, in 1974, ILAIGNAR PERAVAI (Youth Federation) consisting of students and youth was formed to fight for the cause of separate Tamil state. This Federation also pledged its faith in non-violence.

From 1961 to 1972, the demand was only for a Federal status—then the Tamils, forced by Sinhalese fanaticism, are now agitating for a separate sovereign state, which they lovingly call as Tamil Eelam.

AMIRTHALINGAM'S PORTRAYAL

Mr. Amirthalingam, Secretary General of TULF, in his special interview to "THE HINDU" has clearly depicted the evolution of Eelam movement. Following is the text of his depiction :

"When the UNP tried to do something the SLFP opposed it and when the SLFP tried to do something, the UNP opposed it and all our efforts to come to terms with successive Sinhalese Governments failed. Then in 1970, Mrs. Bandaranaika came to power and set up a constituent assembly to draft a new constitution, a republican constitution.

"We put forward certain demands, we did not ask for separation or any such thing. We asked for a federal form of Government and presented a draft Constitution. The Government did not even consider it; they just rejected it off hand. We asked that atleast the Tamil language regulations which had been adopted by the UNP Government earlier be included in the Constitution. The reply we got was there was a specific provision in the Constitution by which, they said, any regulation will not be regarded as part of the Constitution. They specifically saw to it that it was specifically excluded from the ambit of the constitution.

"It was in this situation that all the Tamil parties got together—the Federal party, the All Ceylon Tamil Congress, the Ceylon Workers' Congress of Mr. Thondaman and various other smaller Tamil groups and formed the *Tamil United Front.*

"Even the Tamil United Front never asked for separation at that time. We merely put forward a six-point programme. We asked for justiciable fundamental rights, we asked for the rights of the Tamil language, we asked for decentralisation and autonomy and we asked that the State be made a Secular state, not giving the foremost place to Buddhism.

"The Government of Mrs. Bandaranaika did not even acknowledge the receipt of our letter putting forward these demands. And in this situation, while we were agitating on the basis of these demands, in 1974, the police ran amuck at the World Tamil Research Conference without any provocation. At a meeting where 50,000 people were assembled and a professor from Tiruchi was speaking on Tamil language, the Sinhalese police came on the scene, used teargas and batons and even fired shots. Nine people were killed at the meeting.

SUBJECTED RACE

"It was after that the Tamil people came to the decision that they no longer could live with the Sinhalese and if they could not have even a cultural meeting without having to pay the price of nine people being killed, then they will have to assert their right to be free and independent, which they felt they were historically entitled to demand...

"It was in this situation in 1976 at the first convention of Tamil United Front we decided that we will have as our objective the setting up of an independent Tamil State and we changed the name of Tamil United Front as Tamil United Liberation Front..." (The Hindu, 25th August, 1983).

The TULF has reiterated its faith in democratic means and non-violent methods in achieving its goal even in its Convention held at Mannar on 23rd July, 1983 ! But human beings cannot be all alike !

MILITANT YOUTH

The Tamil youth, who were driven to the verge of frustration decided to take arms—they called themselves "Liberation Tigers".

Another group of youngsters formed Tamil Eelam Liberation Movement—this movement is run mainly by persons who are in "exile".

The LTTE is led by Mr. Prabhakaran, Mr. Balasingam, Mr. Tilagar and others.

The EROS is led by Mr. Rathinasabapathy and Mr. Balakumar.

The TELO is led by Mr. Selvam. Then there is PLOT consisting of the activities of EPRLF. Mr. Madhavan, Mr. Skanda and Mr. Vasudeva play a leading role in these organisations. Mr. Uma Maheswaran and Mr. Padmanabha are the top figures in the PLOT.

Though these organisations rallied under different names

and banners, their objective is the formation of an independent Sovereign Eelam state. Mr. Eelavendan, General Secretary of Tamil Eelam Liberation Front (TELF) has crisply stated his case at Madras on 12th August, 1983. He has stated, "*We do not believe in repairing a rented house. We want to separate Eelem and we would be undeveloped or underdeveloped rather than leave our Homeland to Sinhalese*".

NOTES

Among the members of Liberation organisations, the LTTE led by Mr. Prabhakaran gained momentum both in Sri Lanka and in India. He was spotted for talks by Mr. M.G. Ramachandran, Chief Minister of Tamil Nadu, and Mr. S. Ramachandran (now Food Minister) and was taken to Bangalore when the SAARC meeting was held there during the third week of November, 1986.

LTTE — Liberation Tigers of Tamil Eelam.
TELF — Tamil Eelam Liberation Front.
EROS — Eelam Revolutionary Organisation.
PLOT — People's Liberation Organisation for Tamil Eelam.
EPRLF — Eelam People's Revolutionary Liberation Front.
SAARC — South Asian Association for Regional Co-operation.
TULF — Tamil United Liberation Front.
TELO — Tamil Eelam Liberation Organisation.

3

GENOCIDES GALORE

DURING the past three and half decades since the independence of Sri Lanka, the Tamils in the island have undergone numerous ordeals—their political rights curtailed—their economic status completely shattered—their language relegated to the background—their culture and heritage trodden underneath—Buddhist flag flying atop on many a Hindu temple and Christian Church !

If these ignominies made the Tamils a disgruntled lot, the frequent and brutal onslaughts on them, with the active assistance of the powers-that-be, drove them to the point of demanding a separate sovereign Eelam State !

Here, I have given a list of anti-Tamil riots in Sri Lanka :

1956— Following the introduction of Sinhala only Act, anti-Tamil riots erupted. The Sinhalese leaders made inflammatory speeches with a view to whip up the racial conflagration. The police were only passive onlookers when arson, looting, rape and mass-murders were carried on by the Sinhalese mobs.

1958— Anti-Tamil riots exploded even more violently. Hundreds of Tamils including women and children were massacred and properties of Tamils worth some millions were destroyed.

1961—Peaceful Satyagrahis were arrested, when they protested against the imposition of Sinhala, as the only official language. Hundreds of them were assaulted and tortured by the police and army personnel.

1974—When the Tamil International Research Conference was going on, the police suddenly invaded the venue and nine persons died on the spot.

1977—After the United National Party got into power, anti-Tamil riots erupted again. Security forces openly colluded with the vandals in their acts of arson, rape and murder.

1979—Emergency was declared in Jaffna. Hundreds of Tamil youths were arrested and subjected to inhuman torture. Several youths were massacred.

1981 (May-June)—The Sinhala Police went on a wild rampage indulging in arson in Jaffna. Numerous houses and shops of Tamils were gutted. The famous Tamil Public Library of Jaffna was destroyed. Ten Tamils were killed.

1981—(October) In the violence unleashed, about 200 Tamils lost their lives in Jaffna region. There were sporadic incidents of violence in 1982 and early 1983.

Not only the frequency, but also the brutality is appalling. The following excerpts from *Mr. Tarzia Vittachi's* "Emergency 1958", will clearly depict the brutality.

A high priest of Panandura Hindu temple was dragged out of his temple, beaten to death and burnt in a tar barrel. The belly of a pregnant woman was cut open, the unborn child pulled out and dashed to the ground.

In the Colonisation schemes of D.S. Senanayake, the Sinhalese set fire to sugarcane plantations and drove the Tamils like animals into the conflagration !

The following are the excerpts from *the Sansoni Commission Report (1980)* (*Courtesy, from "Genocide of Tamils in Sri Lanka"* published by the People's Liberation Organisation of Tamil Eelam) :

Mr. Ignatius, the owner of the biggest shop in Alawa, which was run by that family for two generations, was killed in these attacks. He was battered and while still alive, coconut oil was poured on him, straw was heaped on him, and he was set on fire.

In Kantalai there was evidence of gruesome murder of three members of a Tamil family including a four-year-old child who was snatched from the arms of his father, stabbed on the back with a sword and heartlessly thrown into a blazing house.

RAPE

Six daughters of one Ramaswamy Pillai were raped by a gang of 30 persons in Matale.

About 200 to 250 cases of rape were led in evidence before the commission. The victims were innocent Tamil estate workers and the attackers were from adjoining Sinhala villages. The police personnel failed to arrest the offenders even when they were identified and their names and addresses were given.

ARSON AND LOOTING

At Kakirawa the business known as "Subramaniams", which was a business carried on in that area for generations by a Tamil family was completely destroyed, looted and burnt. This was a very large business and the estimated loss is to the tune of 5 crores of rupees.

DAMAGE TO HINDU TEMPLE

Sithivinayar temple, Katugastota, has been in existence for 50 years...They broke open the gate and broke the idols. The attackers took another idol of Siva and threw it on the road and spat on it and kicked it...The entire temple was broken down... The temple priest was assaulted.

AMNESTY INTERNATIONAL

Again during 1981, *the Amnesty International* received reports of violation of human rights—in particular, arbitrary arrests and detention and the use of torture and third-degree methods—being carried out by the security forces of Sri Lanka Government. Subsequently a Mission was sent to the island for investigation. Here are the findings of the Mission :

In all the cases investigated, arrests of suspects had been carried out by large contingents of army and police who did not identify themselves, did not show an arrest warrant and did not inform relatives present at the time of arrest of the grounds for arrest; nor had they informed the relatives subsequently of the whereabouts of the persons arrested or the reasons for their continued detention.

Access to lawyers and relatives is denied as a matter of official policy to those detained under the Prevention of Terrorism Act. Persons arrested had been held incommunicado for prolonged periods, and access to lawyers had been denied for at least four months and in most cases, for nine months from the date of arrest. Relatives of those arrested have in most cases been denied access, in some cases for more than a year. Five persons, for example, had been held in solitary confinement for more than eight months after arrest.

Despite specific legal and constitutional safeguards, torture was reported to have been utilised both in army camps and by the police, mostly by the army. The reported methods included prolonged beatings on many parts of the body, hanging individuals upside down, inserting needles under toes and fingernails, placing of chilli powder into sensitive parts of the body, forcing the drinking of salted water, assault on sexual organs and extracting "confessions".

Despite verdicts of homicide being returned by the magistrate of Jaffna in at least four cases of killings by the security forces, as of December 1982, no independent or official investigations have been instituted by the Government. Nor have any criminal prosecutions been instituted.

Detenus in army custody are reported to be in poor physical conditions of detention. Several are kept chained to the wall, in poor hygienic conditions and without exercise. Reading and writing materials have been continuously denied. Individuals have complained of serious restrictions on food and water and of physical assault by the authorities and of difficulties in obtaining medical treatment, when required.

In several cases, detenus were prevented from approaching the Advisory Board by officials, who had professed ignorance of the board's existence.

INHUMAN TORTURE

The Amnesty International recorded evidence in more than 20 cases—in all cases, the Tamils, in the pretext of enforcing law were subjected to inhuman torture. One such case, I am quoting verbatim.

The following account was given to the delegation by a former detainee under the Prevention of Terrorism Act who had been arrested on 16 November 1981 and who reported being tortured on the day of his arrest and during the following 10 days :

"When I was being taken to Mankumal Army Camp, they put about 10 to 15 army helmets on my head. While I was carrying this heavy load, they told me to balance a 45 litre plastic barfel of water. This continued for about one hour. If I failed to keep up the can, I was assaulted...At about 11.00 p.m., we arrived at Gurunagar Army Camp in Jaffna...A man who told me he was a corporal brought a needle and pricked me with it.

"Two or three men were holding me at the time. They were all in civilian clothes. They inserted needles in the muscles of my arm and under my fingernails. They also pierced the underside of my arm. They took a thread which they put under the tendon and pulled it through backwards and forwards while asking me questions about terrorist leaders.

"Then they handcuffed me and tied me with my right hand

and my right leg to a wooden bench. In that position I was allowed to sleep. I got food the next day. I was taken for further interrogation to an office. One army Captain conducted the investigations and one other man in civilian clothes was also there...during that interrogation I was not assaulted. Then I was taken outside to the verandah, where there is a concrete platform, three or four feet high. I was told to lie down on that platform, face downwards. I lay down on the platform, from my feet to the waist the top of my body hanging outside. An army man in civilian clothes kicked me with an iron pipe on the soles of my feet.

"The pain was like an electric current. Some 10 other people stood around, all were in civilian dress. After that they put broken glass on the concrete floor, on which I was told to kneel down with my hand put above my head. When I was about to fall, they put me up again in the same position, beating me. After that, they brought chillis in powdered form which they stuffed into my nostrils...They stuffed it in my nostrils with a nail so that it entered my forehead. This happened while I was still kneeling on the glass.

"At one time, they recorded my statement and got my signature. I am unable to say whether the statement was in English or in Sinhala, but it was not in Tamil. I was not aware what I signed". (Courtesy—Article of NITHEN BELLE in "INDIAN EXPRESS", dated 14th Aug. 1983).

LIBERATION TIGERS

The Liberation Tigers, Kuttimani and Jegannathan, who were killed later on, (on July 23, 1983) during the Welikade prison massacre, gave their evidence before the High Court of Colombo. The tales divulged by them are most gruesome and heart-rending.

KUTTIMANI, during his evidence, described how he was kicked, beaten and boxed—how chilly fume was used on him—how a rod was thrust into his anus!

JEGANNATHAN stated that he also was tortured. Urine was

given when he asked for water. Several Tamil youths had been kept in dark cells, subjected to electric shocks, water jets, light streams, burning with cigarette butts, pins in fingernails, whipping, baton charges, head hung down from roof tops. Every imaginable torture had been inflicted on the Tamil youths. (From the proceedings of the High Court, Colombo).

Such repressive and agonising tortures, coupled with repeated attacks on Tamils forced them to think in the line of separation. They began to think that unless Tamils got independence, they would be completely annihilated! What is wrong in their logic ?

They sincerely feel that their's is a cause of liberation—not separation—that too, arising out of frustration, and as the only panacea for all the ills that the Tamils have been undergoing in Sri Lanka during the past !

NOTES

Amnesty International released an 89 page report on 8th September, 1986, detailing 272 instances of "people reported to have been seized by the country's security forces over the past 20 months"...

The organisation also accuses the Sri Lanka Government of systematic human rights abuses since late 1984, and says the suspension of safeguards under emergency rule have encourged security forces to think that they can get away with abuses.

The report contains several affidavits and international press reports about the atrocities.

The report says that many were shot on the spot, but some forty 18-25 year olds were taken to the cemetery at Thambulivil where they were ordered to dig their own graves and shot.

The report also says the headmaster of a methodist orphange who reported the disappearance of some 23 young men was charged with "spreading false rumours and false statements". Subsequently the Court acquitted him.

4

RECENT DEVIL DANCE

SRI LANKA, a strife-torn island since the mid 50s of this century, saw the worst of its kind during the last week of July, 1983.

Ever since December 1982, when Mr. Jayawardene's UNP, through a referendum, secured an extension of 6 years tenure, the political sky of Sri Lanka was not calm ! The wind was heavy, clouds gathering, all portending the onset of a gale !

The Tamils, disgruntled because of the constant discriminations, finding that their talks with the Government could not ameliorate their conditions because the Sinhalese leaders never kept up their assurances, were much bewildered and enthusiastic among them ingratiated into the movement of TIGERS !

The Prevention of Terrorism Act of 1981, instead of cowing down the Tamils, made them infuriated and they, with much more vigour began to advocate the cause of separate Eelam—this cause gathered momentum, day by day !

The TULF, which had been known as Tamil United Front till 1976, advocating Federal status to the Tamils, was forced in that year to raise its banner for a separate Eelam ! The wedge between the Tigers and TULF was very thin—that too as regards the means ! The tigers put their faith in taking to arms, while the TULF, even in its Conference at Talai Mannar on 23rd July, 1983, reiterated its faith in Parliamentary democracy and advocated only non-violent means for achieving its aspired goals !

This July 23, 1983 was a day of three important events in the annals of Sri Lanka. That was the day in which TULF decided at Talai Mannar, not to participate in future, in any of the conferences, convened by the government of Mr. Jayawardene—this is the outcome of the frustration arising of their past, bitter experience !

Again this July 23, 1983, was the sixth anniversary of Mr. Jayawardene's rule in Sri Lanka.

On the same day, 13 army men were killed in an ambush, allegedly by liberation Tigers or some such terrorists ! It is generally known fact that this was a sequel of the rape of 4 Tamils, all inmates of a hostel, by army men and among them 2 committed suicide subsequently. Though this is dismissed by the authorities as a 'mere story', there are evidences to show that the rape actually took place and only the culprits concerned were attacked in this ambush !

Mr. Ashish Ray has written in "Sunday", that "*while this (ambush against army men) was probably an important spark that has set off the conflagration, what has not come to light is the possibility of an outrage by soldiers on a girls' college in Tinnavely in Jaffna in the last week of July*".

This ambush of July 23 resulted in an outbreak of violence in the island—the dimension of which is unheard of in the annals of the world, with the only exception of atrocities perpetrated by Nazis in the concentration camps !

The orgy of violence let loose devoured more than 2,500 lives and more than a lakh of persons were rendered homeless ! How many women were raped, nobody knows ! The estimated loss due to the organised looting and arson goes upto Rs. 2000 crores—what more intriguing is the Police and the army personnel, instead of putting down the violence, remained as silent spectators and in many cases, they are alleged to have been even active participants !

Not only that ! The notorious kawk in the Cabinet, *Mr. Cyril Mathew* was seen in so many places in Colombo, kindling the fire, encouraging publicly the looting Sinhalese mobs ! It looked as though it was a well-planned attack, very cruelly and callously executed, with the connivance and shelter of the powers-that-be !

The proclamation of Emergency and the imposition of curfew coupled with the enormous powers conferred on the army and also the strict censorship rules, all these things were effectively made use of by the Government and the world is denied of the full picture of the orgy !

We are having only the leaked-out news and the evidences of the persons, lucky enough to escape from the brutal massacre, and also the reports of the foreign correspondents; but they themselves, are enough to understand the brutality of the attack against the Tamils ! Here are some such narrations regarding the riots—only samples are given—because full coverage is an impossibility.

JUNGLE LAW

A group of people from Colombo landed at Trivandrum on July 29, 1983. They said, "It is a Jungle law there ! No place is safe and Tamil word uttered at a public place can mean you death or torture".

Messrs. Natarajan, Paul Pandian and Rajachoodamani, were partners in a hardware business in Colombo. Their native place is Tiruchendur, Tamil Nadu. They also arrived in the same flight. They lost all their properties, worth about Rs. 30 lakhs and naturally they looked dazed ! "We are lucky to be alive", they said.

Most of the repatriates seemed to be scared, even after landing in India. They were reluctant to reveal their identity fearing retaliation against their friends and relatives stranded in Colombo till then.

According to two persons belonging to Chettinad employed in the "Free trade zone" in Colombo, the Tamils in Sri Lanka were identified from the voters' list and attacked. Their properties were first looted and then the houses were set on fire.

Some narrated the gruesome story of having been fleeced by the Sinhalese even when they were fleeing for their lives. They said that people fleeing the Sri Lankan Capital to the airport were those who faced death. "Bands of armed Sinhalese stop the cars and buses and loot them. The Sinhalese taxi-drivers fleece the Tamilian passengers. The minimum rate to cover the 42 km run is Rs. 1,000 if the passengers included men and women", they told.

VIOLIN ONLY SAVED !

Mrs. M.L. Vasanthakumari, a noted Tamil Singer had gone over to Sri Lanka. Unfortunately she and her troupe were caught in the muddle. After three days of "total confinement" in a five-star hotel in Colombo, this troupe arrived at Madras on 29th July, almost on the verge of collapse ! A member of the troupe told, "All our belongings were looted, we remained shut in our room without a dress to change. We have lost even our chappals and landed on our soil bare-foot ! I always carry my violin with me and so it is safe. All other instruments, including Mrudangam, are lost."

COLOMBO BURNING

"Colombo is burning ! We saw it !" said a passenger who returned to Madras on 30th July by an IA flight.

A passenger belonging to a 9 member group which had gone to Colombo for shooting a film said, "We have come back alive —that is enough to make the people in India understand the ordeal we and other people of Tamil origin underwent in the past few days in Colombo. From the hotel opposite to Ramakrishna Math in Wellavettai, where we stayed, we saw buildings and shops burning, columns of smoke leaping on three sides, on the fourth side, there was only the sea !" He also told that the telephone in the hotel did not work. With great difficulty they could contact an official of the Indian High Commission and ask him help. But the official told them that the families of High Commission officials themselves were confined to their houses. The officials, however, advised the members of their troupe to lock their rooms inside and remain there till help arrived !

Mr. Venkat, a Tamil film director, was chased at Colombo on 26th July by the Sinhalese mob and was cruelly done to death on the road and the police and soldiers silently witnessed, even enjoyed the scene, one person described !

Mr. Subbiah Pillai (age 53) who had been living in Sri Lanka for the past 40 years, said that he sought asylum in the third floor of a hotel in Kaisar St. in Colombo, during the riots. According to him, 100 Tamils were arrayed opposite to that hotel, all their hands having been tied backwards. All these persons were shot dead ! The Sinhalese, after committing this dastardly act, danced over the dead bodies ! Some of them used bayonets to ascertain whether any of them was left alive ! Mr. Subbiah Pillai told that he had lost about 20 lakhs worth of properties and returned to homeland, penniless !

Beggar too joined the Fray

One Rengaswamy (45) working in a tea estate in Bantarawella, 150 km from Colombo, said (on August 4, 1983), "Every incident we saw on the night of July 25/26 will remain in our minds !" He describes how troublesome was his train travel. When the train stopped at one station, he said, "We saw two Sinhalese attacking a Tamil aged about 50 with bottles. The man died on the spot soon. Thereafter half a dozen persons joined the 'killers', who came towards us...The 21 repatriates in a compartment had to swallow insults hurled by the Sinhalese. Even a beggar joined the clan and started abusing the Tamils.

Some people snatched the handbags from women." Mr. Kanakaraj and Mr. Meyyappan, who also came along with him, corroborated his version.

Mrs. Selvamany Ganesan, 36 years old mother of three, who survived the Badulla massacre told "The Guardian", through an interpreter on July 27, that a crowd had attacked the house of a neighbour named Ramanathan, a camphor dealer. His 15 years old son, who had climbed on the roof of their house was shot by a soldier and fell on the ground. Mrs. Ganesan fled with her children to her aunt's house nearby. There she heard firing outside and then explosion. The house in which they took shelter was also set on fire. She fled with her children down a lane at the back of this house. She saw pools of blood. On the main road in front of Ramanathan's house, there was a pile of bodies including those of her husband, brother-in-law, father-in-law and her sister-in-law's husband. They all appeared to have received gunshot wounds.

The manager of a big jewellery shop at Grandpass, Colombo arrived at Trichy on 7th August, 1983. While narrating his story, he preferred anonymity. He told that the shop in which he was working was looted by 50 armed Sinhalese, while half a dozen army men were standing guard of the operation looting. He said that the Tamils in Kandy and other places were still "in the grip of fear".

BUDDHIST FLAG ON THE TEMPLE TOP

Another youth, a native of Mannachanallur, Trichy Dt. who also came down by the same flight, was running a hardware shop at Kandy. He said that his shop was completely looted and only by God's grace, he could escape. He also said that Muthumariamman temple at Mattalai had been ransacked by the Sinhalese mobs. The idols in the temple were broken to pieces. The temple care had been burnt down and the calf elephant had been driven away. At last, Buddhist flag had been hoisted on the top of the temple. Another man, who also came by this plane from Colombo, told the reporter of the *Indian Express,* that it was a multi-pronged attack on Tamils—by army, navy, air force, police personnel along with Sinhalese criminals (*Indian Express,* Angust 18, 1983).

Mr. J. Ramaswamy (60) a native of Turaiyur in Trichy District, who was having a flour mill, besides a pawn broker shop in Hatton said (August 19) that on the night of July 24, rioting Sinhalese mobs threw "petrol bombs" on all shops, houses and industrial premises of Tamils. He said one Ponnuswamy, a native of Turaiyur and proprietor of Liberty Theatre in Hatton was alone in house after sending his family to his friend's house for safety and he was cut to pieces by the Sinhalese mob.

On the night of 25 July, one Palaniandi (60), a native of a village near Mettupalayam, Trichy District was butchered at Colombo. This news was conveyed to his wife by his relatives of Colombo, now staying in one of the refugee camps.

A middle-aged man, a Tamil of Indian origin, who had settled in Colombo two decades back, flew to Madras on 16th August, 1983. He told *The Hindu* correspondent, "We have seen the army and the Navy personnel walk into Indian's homes and take away unmarried girls in government vehicles. Hundreds of school and college girls of Indian origin have been raped ! What is their future ? Should we not hang our heads in shame ?" he asked. He also said, "We are leaderless and looked to the Indian Government to ensure our protection by taking up our cause with the Sri Lanka Government. At least for the time being a U.N. peace-keeping force is a must." (*The Hindu*)

VILLAGE BURNT

According to a report that reached London on 28th July, the whole village of Velvettithurai, native place of Kuttimani (Tiger who was done to death in Welikade prison) was ransacked—A number of Tamils were shot dead—No house in the village remains unburnt !

Mr. Thanjai Ramamurthy, Vice-president of Kamaraj Congress, returned from Colombo on 30th July, 1983, after attending Talai Mannar conference of TULF as a special invitee. He told that on 24th morning he got the information that Mr. Kala Parameswaran, a University Professor and his father-in-law had been shot dead on 23rd night, while they were sleeping in the house at Jaffna. Mr. Ramamurthy also got the information that the house of Mr. Sivachidaram MP (TULF) at Colombo was ransacked, all the valuables were looted and then the house was set on fire !

A five-star hotel in Triconamalee was completely pulled down. This belongs to a Tamilian.

Mr. Sigamani, brother-in-law of Thangadurai, a Tiger butchered in Welikade prison and the District Secretary of Madras District Rationalist Forum, had been to Sri Lanka during July, 1983. He said that his friend Mr. Sundararajan was fired at by the Sinhalese mob and he sustained a bleeding injury on his left eye ! The rioters could not get petrol immediately and that is why Mr. Sundararajan could escape with this injury.

RAPE

According to Mr. Sigamani, one Ramanathan and his father were tied with rope by the Sinhalese mob. Ramanathan's two sisters were stripped naked, raped by at least a dozen persons under their very nose. Then they severed the heads of these two girls and butchered Ramanathan and his father !

When Mr. Sigamani was staying in the house of one of his friends, he saw soldiers entered the house of one Mr. Kathamuthu. His unmarried daughter forcefully taken to the truck, where she was raped by them. Then she was pushed out from the truck and she died !

Mr. Malaikutti, younger brother of a Tiger by name Raju Pillai was shot dead by army men and his body was thrown into a well.

Messrs. Abdul Razak, Mohamed Ghouse, Sheik Dawood and Abdul Hameed, all natives of Karaikal went on tour to Sri

Lanka, during the outbreak of riots. The lodge in which they stayed in Colombo was completely damaged. They saw a newly-wed couple, going in a car, was stopped by the Sinhalese mob and both of them were burnt alive.

One Dharmalingam of Turaiyur, Trichy District, who had been to Sri Lanka on tour was staying in the house of one Chelliah, his friend in Kottanchenai near Colombo. He saw the Sinhalese mob entering a number of houses and butchering the inmates—the victims were Tamils. Mr. Chelliah led Mr. Dharmalingam to the house of a Muslim friend. From there he could see the most horrible and breath-taking incident. The one year old child of Mr. Chelliah was thrown hither and thither by the Sinhalese like a ball and one of them squeezed its neck—then the child was trampled by another person. Mr. Chelliah and his wife also were butchered in the cold-blooded manner !

Mr. Kamalasekaran of Ariyalur in Trichy District, returning to Trichy on 7th August told that he saw that 6 members of a Tamil family were tied to the lamp posts and brutally done to death at Colombo on 24th July. Though he miraculously escaped, he was having burn injuries all over his body and also having a bandage on his left leg ! He was staying in Greenland Hotel in Colombo. All the Tamils who were found inside this hotel were butchered like goats and the hotel itself was set on fire !

Dr. Srinivasan (47) working in the Leprosy Centre of Colombo said that he was attacked by the Sinhalese with dangerous weapons like crowbars. His car was completely smashed. On coming to know that he was a Medical officer, the Armymen came to his rescue !

Mr. T.R. Janardanam, MLC, who leads the TULF at Madras told the press reporters on 14th August, 1983, that he had received information about the attack of Sinhalese mob on Mr. Chelliah Kumarasurier, Tele-communication Minister in the Srimao Bandaranaika Cabinet. This former minister received as many as 24 injuries, in spite of his entreaties that he had nothing to do with the Eelam demand. According to his information, Brig. Thambiah, a Tamil army officer and his Sinhalese wife were done to death. The house of Bastia Pillai, Chief Investigating Officer of violent activities of Tamil Tigers, was also razed.

Sarathas, a Tamil owned shop at the Fort area in the heart of Colombo, had rolled down its shutters as soon as the violence spread. The Sinhalese mob stopped an electricity department truck passing by, pulled out the driver and then drove it into the shop, shattering the shutter. The shop was set aflame, after looting it clean.

BUTCHER STALLS AND SEVERED TAMIL HEADS

"Tamil Meat available"—this sort of announcements could be seen in a number of butcher stalls in Colombo on 26th and 27th July. In some of them severed heads of Tamilians were exhibited. It seemed as if the land of Buddhists turned into a land of Cannibals !

When Mr. Gopalaswamy MP (DMK) met some of the refugees in Mandapam camp, some of them told heart-rending stories. According to them two girls of one Diraviyam Nadar, a vessel merchant, were studying in a Buddhist School in Thembattakudai near Colombo. *Both these girls were raped by the Buddhist Priests themselves and* they were sent off. The irony is that only recently Mr. Diraviyam Nadar, father of those girls, had donated Rs. 20,000 to that Buddhist institution.

Mr. M.P. Velu (45) of Salem, a driver of Anna Transport Corporation had been to Ceylon to see some of his relatives there. He also sustained injury during the violence. Subsequently he was taken to the Government hospital, Nuera Eliya. He had been asked to act like a dumb man in the event of being questioned by any body. There he saw a lady doctor (Tamilian) being brutally attacked by Sinhalese, when she was actually examining a patient. She died on the spot. This Mr. Velu also saw a van in which the dead body of a naked Tamil woman was hung upside down, on its backside. The van was near the Radio Station. Some police and army men were standing guard.

of this body and some were taking tea in a nearby Tea-stall. Mr. Velu, on enquiries, was informed that with this dead body, the van was driven from village to village and "Exhibition March" covered a distance of roughly 100 miles.

After the riots, writes the correspondent of *The Week*, "The capital wears the sombre look of a vast cemetery. Streets are still littered with debris, but half burnt bodies have been removed and buried...Tamils are nowhere seen during times of curfew relaxation. They have either fled to refugee camps run by the government and religious institutions or gone out of the country. They knew they were not safe once it became clear to all that Sinhalese youths were carrying voters lists for marking out Tamil homes for their arson spree."

Mrs. Anita Pratap of *Sunday* gives a more touching description. She has written, "This correspondent left Colombo with the feeling that racial prejudice had gone beyond the point of return. The Sinhalese and the Tamils cannot live together in amity ever again ! The scars are far too deep and the mistrust far too keenly entrenched. The Tamils of Sri Lanka are a spurned lot, spurned by their own government. How can they live in security in a country where the president has told foreign correspondents (to *Sunday Observer* of London) that he did not care about the Tamils ?..."

5

EYE WITNESSES ABROAD

THE overwhelming evidence of the Tamils, who by God's grace could escape the wrath of the ruthless Sinhalese mob, may perhaps be dismissed as exaggerated versions by those perched up in gadi in Sri Lanka.

As a matter of fact, the reports of all the Indian pressmen may be dubbed as 'prejudiced', or 'biased'. But the eye-witness accounts of the foreigners, who have got no prejudice or predilection, cannot be so easily dismissed. Here are some among them :

A Norwegian, who returned to Oslo on 29th July, (1983) *Mrs. Skarstein* said she saw 20 Tamils burnt to death in their mini bus, after it was set on fire by the looters. She told the newspaper "VERDENS GANG", that she saw the burning on her way to the international airport of Colombo. She stated, "A mini-bus full of Tamils was stopped by the Sinhalese, who poured petrol over it and set it on fire. All the doors were kept closed... and 20 Tamils were burnt to death". She described the capital as an inferno. According to her there were burning houses everywhere and the target of attack was only the Tamils !

The West German eye witnesses of the violence on 26th July referred to it as *"a wave of blood lust"* by the Sinhalese against the Tamils.

Holiday makers who returned to Dusseldorff on 28th July, said that hundreds of Tamils had been murdered and even their hotel waiters told them proudly and gleefully, "We have killed several of them !"

According to "The Guardian", several European tourists in Colombo saw (on 28th July) nine Tamils burnt alive at Colombo's main railway station. All nine died under horrific and agonising circumstances. These reports were later confirmed by the Colombo police. According to the special correspondent of "The Guardian", "The men, after being beaten up by the Sinhalese mob, were tied down on the railway track by the crowed. Using papers and other debris as kindering material, they set fire to the horribly battered, but still living people. They died in a few minutes".

HONEY-MOONER

A British tourist returned (on 28th July) from Sri Lanka, where he had gone over to enjoy honey-moon. He said, "There were gangs of looters in Colombo. It was quite frightening. We saw lots of shops and buildings on fire and people staggering through the streets with as much as they could carry from looted shops."

According to the Colombo correspondent of "The Times", (on 29th July) a Tamil youngman, who was travelling in a train, was pursued by the Sinhalese mob from carriage to carriage and finally pummelled and beaten until he died, naked and bleeding.

Mr. Alan Gates, a teacher with the British Council, returned from Colombo on 5th August. He said that while he and a friend of him were on a beach, in their bid to escape the violence, they saw smoke billowing from behind nearly trees and were told that a Tamil house had been set on fire. Shortly afterwards they say boys walking away from the scene clutching boxes of goods looted from the building.

TAMILS ANNIHILATED

Mr. Jaweed Jaffar, a former newsman of Pakistan flew to Singapore on 28th July. He stated that the Sinhalese action was aimed at annihilating the Tamils. He could secure a taxi from the hotel only after proving that he was not a Tamilian. On his way to the airport, the Sinhalese taxi-driver told him "you see, we have completely annihilated the Tamils."

Mrs. Renald Libro, a teacher of West Germany had been to Sri Lanka on tour. On her return to Bonn, she told that she saw a number of Tamils being butchered, and also a number of Tamil women raped by the Sinhalese. She said, "I was also chased by a mob, I had to run to a police station. The police, instead of giving me protection, drove me out at the point of bayonet !"

Mr. Garry of California (US) had been to Sri Lanka on tour, alongwith his wife. He returned to Madras on August 3 and told the reporters that he and his wife were attacked by the mob while they were travelling in a car in Colombo. They had to flee for their lives and when they reached the US High Commission, they saw there 10 Tamils with serious injuries. These Tamils narrated how cruelly they were attacked by the Sinhalese mob. He said "Sri Lanka seems to be a cemetery and if this continues, we can see no Tamilian alive in Sri Lanka and we are still in the grip of fear !"

The above testimonies, though only few in number, are enough to depict the sordid state of affairs that prevailed in Sri Lanka during the last of July, 1983. It may rightly be described a week of blood-shed in the annals of Sri Lanka !

6

MASSACRE IN WELIKADE PRISON

THE orgy of violence let loose on the innocent Tamils could not be stopped even by strongly built prison walls. Prison bars also were broken and the guards are said to be helpless !

The mad attack took place on the night of July 25 at Welikade Prison in Colombo. During this attack, 35 Tamil prisoners were done to death.

Two young Tamil students—*Anbazhagan* and *Mayilvahanan* both 16 years old—who had no involvement in any movement whatsoever, were cruelly stabbed. Two famous Liberation Tigers, *Kuttimani* and *Jagan* were the main target of attack.

How the attack emanated, how the occurrence took place all these things are not at all given proper explanation by the persons perched in power.

When asked about this gruesome massacre *Mr. Jayasinghe*, Foreign Secretary of Sri Lanka Government told the correspondents at Madras (on 27th July, 1983) that there was hand-to-hand" fighting and no weapon was used. This is another instance to show how callous the Sinhalese are towards the Tamils—his version is nothing but utter falsehood. The whole machinery of the Sinhalese Government was upto do anything against the Tamils—hush up things when glaring instances of inhuman acts were pointed out—shift the burden to anybody and so on.

Contrary to the version of Mr. Jayasinghe, the Chief Warden of Welikade Prison, Mr. Karunaratne told before the inquiry that *Tamils were beaten and stabbed to death*! How could persons be stabbed to death in a hand-to-hand fight ?

According to Mr. Karunaratne, hundreds of Sinhalese prisoners broke out of their cells to attack the Tamils. He also told that prison authorities had information that a second attack might take place after July 25, alongwith a jail break, but he could not act in time.

The Daily News quoted him as saying that about 300 to 400 prisoners armed with poles, iron rods, sticks and axes, had invaded the wing where the Tamils were being held. He said that the prisoners surrounded him and snatched the keys of the cells from him !

How is it that the prisoners were armed with such dangerous weapons ? How could they get those weapons when they were put behind the bars ? How did they break open their cells ? All these pertinent questions are left unanswered. The occurrence took place during dead night and so the assailants could not be identified, not all of them, of course ! But at least some among them could be identified but no such attempt was made on the part of the Government, either to identify the culprits or to book to them under penal law !

There is an honest doubt among the intelligentsia that the assailants could have been the army men and police personnel of the Sri Lanka Government and not some of the prisoners as told by the Government officials.

If only the prisoners attacked the Tamil prisoners, it is logical to infer that only Sinhalese could have attacked them! If so, how many of them were then in the custody ? Will not the jail records speak to it ? No ! The Sri Lanka Government was not prepared to come forward with true facts, because if truth comes trickling, it would expose its carefully staged conspiracy, so callously executed !

Mr. David Beresford, a special correspondent of "The Guardian" (London, 13th August 1983) wrote, "The two men, Sellarasa 'Kuttimani' Yogendran, Leader of Tamil Eelam Liberation Front (T.E.L.F.) and Ganeshnathan Jeganathan, a political writer, had been sentenced to death last year... In speeches from the dock, the two men announced that they would donate their eyes in the hope that they would be grafted on to Tamils who would see the birth of Eelam, the independent Tamil State they were fighting for.

"The second hand reports from Batticoloa Jail, where the survivors of Welikade massacre are now being kept, say that the *two men were forced to kneel and their eyes were gouged out with iron bars before they were killed.* One VERSION has it that Kuttimani's tongue was cut out by an attacker who drank his blood and cried '*I drank the blood of a Tiger*'."

To the assailants the blood of Sellarasa Kuttimani was so sweet and delicious and they were so blood-thirsty !

To them, his tongue, which was responsible for delivering from the dock, a Demosthenes like oration, was fit to be served from his mouth! Or did they feel that like the wounds of Caesar, his tongue was capable of oration even after his demise ?

To them, the eyes which longed for seeing Eelam severed of its shackles, should be trodden underneath beyond recognition ! Did they fear that those eyes, if left intact, would achieve the goal of this Tiger ?

The history has never seen an act which can any way be compared with this beastly behaviour !

In spite of this, the Sri Lanka government has not uttered a word of sympathy—even lip sympathy—to the victims of such unheard of orgy !

We, the Tamils, shed tears of blood on hearing this notorious episode ! July 25 will ever be painfully remembered by all Tamils—will be written as a Horror Day in the annals of the world! or a Black Day !

If Bastille Prison acquired historical importance during the French Revolution of 1789, Welikade Prison has attracted more attention and acquired more importance and it will ever be remembered by the posterity !

In Bastille, the prisoners were freed on July 14, by the revolutionaries—but in Welikade the prisoners were done to death like mad dogs.

ANOTHER HORROR DAY

The Horror Day of July 25 was over, taking away the lives of 35 Tamils ! But the horror was not over.

Two days later (27th July) another 17 persons were killed in the same prison. This time *Dr. Rajasundaram* and *Mr. S.A. David (both of them Gandhian leaders) two Catholic* priests and one Methodist Minister were among those murdered.

These persons had been removed into a padlocked hall immediately after July 25 killings. They were convinced that further attacks were coming and so made repeated requests to the prison authorities on July 26 for better security measures. The authorities were kind enough to give assurances—but they were of no avail. In the language of the Sinhalese assurances are given only to see that they are never kept up, be it an assurance from an ordinary official or from a person adoring the gadi of a President !

By about 2-30 AM on July 27, hearing the screaming and whistling outside, one of the priests looked out of the high window. To his horror, he saw persons breaking from a neighbouring compound, wielding axes, iron bars, pieces of firewood and sticks. There was no sign of prison guards.

The mob had already killed some prisoners in the downstairs cell. It ran up the hall and began breaking the padlock. Dr. Rajasundaram then went to the door and cried "why are you trying to kill us ? What have we done to you ?'

At that moment the door burst open and Dr. Rajasundaram was hit on his neck with a lengthy iron rod. Blood spurted several feet. With him, other eight persons also died on the spot.

One of the prisoners who survived in this attack told the correspondent of *The Guardian* (*Mr. Beresford*) later, "At this juncture we thought that we should defend ourselves. We broke the two tables in the hall and took the legs to defend ourselves. We kept them at bay. They threw bricks at us. We threw them back. Pieces of firewood and iron bars were thrown on us. We used them to defend ourselves. And it went on for about half an hour. *They shouted, 'you are the Priests ! We must kill you'*.

Leave alone the horrible attack. What is the meaning of their shouting? Does it not mean that they were not only hooligans but also hirelings, engaged by some unseen hands for this heinous purpose?

Of course, an inquest was done—but these details did not emerge ! Prison Wardens claim that the keys to the cell were stolen from them. Were they stolen or forcefully taken? Two versions are there and which of them is correct ?

No, nothing can be more correct than to say that this dastardly act was perpetrated by those at power with a vile motive of annihilating the Tamil leaders !

Lawyers who appeared for the prisoners categorically accused the Wardens of having participated in the murderous attacks. The lawyers also claim that they were not given opportunity to bring evidence inspite of the representations to the Government!

A government with clean hands would have permitted these

lawyers to let in evidence in their favour and establish their case but we cannot expect the Government of Mr. Jayawardene to do so since its hands are soaked in blood !

But for the despatch of Mr. Beresford of "the Guardian", the above facts could not have been brought to light. The Government would have as usual dismissed these things as mere "fictions" and "imaginations". The whole of Tamil community and also the ardent lovers of human rights and dignity are greatly indebted to him.

MAD DOGS

At this juncture one is prone to recall a notorious remark of *Mr. Cyril Mathews,* Sri Lanka Minister, *"Terrorism cannot be stopped and has never been stopped by means of law. Terrorism has been stopped by terrorism. In no other way it is possible. Terrorists have to be killed because they are terrorists. They are like mad dogs and no better than that* !

Mr. Cyril Mathews is known to be a hawk and his "sermon" could have naturally incited the Sinhalese! And what more can Tamils expect from the Government in which this hawk is capable of pulling the wire and commanding army.

He dubbed the "terrorists" as mad dogs and the prisoners in Welikade prison also were done to death like mad dogs. Does it not show that the Sri Lanka government has direct hand in the gruesome massacre ?

7

ANTI-INDIAN OVERTONE

"OVERNIGHT, the prosperous and industrial Tamil community of Sri Lanka, a section of which controls Sri Lankan trade and business, was reduced to the status of refugees, stripped clean of all its belongings and fruits of years of honest labour. Even though there have been cases of Tamils' eyes being gouged out, people being disembowelled, children being dismembered and men being roasted alive, the emphasis in the atrocities has been not to kill, but to plunder. Death is not the real punishment meted out to the Tamils. There seems to have been a systematic effort to humiliate and subjugate them, reduce them to pauperty so that their tormentors could bulldoze themselves to a position of strength. There was an organised attempt to shatter the economic foundations of the Tamil community. This time the rich Tamils too, like Gnanam, Maharajas and Thillainathams who control the textile and trade industries, reeled under the onslaught. Hitherto the anti-Tamil riots that foster perpetually in the northern and eastern provinces spilled to the capital, Colombo, as well as other places like Kandy, Anuradhapura and Ratnapura. *It was a country-wide destruction of Tamils as a race. As the looting, arson and massacres continued against the Tamils, it became broad based to include all Indians, not just*

Tamils". Thus wrote Mrs. Anita Pratap in "Sunday" special issue.

This time, the Sindhis, Marwaris and Bohra businessmen, all suffered in the orgy of the Sinhalese vandalism. This time, this anti-Indian sentiment was very marked—the impact too was very high.

Otherwise, why should the officials of the Indian High Commission also be attacked ?

Mr. Iyer, Mr. Abraham, members of the Indian mission staff were brutally attacked during the curfew hours, when they were going to their office. Mr. Iyer was dragged out of his car. His identity card was of no use. In spite of showing this card, he was beaten with iron rods, chased and kicked by a gang of about 25 Sinhala youths. One of Mr. Iyer's eyes has been seriously affected. Several bandages had to be put all over his body. Mr. P.V. Narasimha Rao, External Affairs Minister, took him to Delhi on the pretext of affording him adequate medical attention but ostensibly to avoid embarrassment !

Mr. Mohana Chandran, also a member of the mission, was unfortunate enough to have his house completely looted and burnt. He and his wife had been for shopping during the looting spree and that is why they could escape. But the tragedy was that they had nothing left except the clothes they were wearing!

The above said acts themselves are enough to warrant a stern action from India, but for the reasons best known to them the Indian government was "over-cautious", according to Mr. G.K. Reddy. This is, in spite of the fact that about 20 Indian High Commission staff with their families, had to be placed in expensive hotels for security reasons!

PHOBIA OF JRJ

It seems JRJ has been groping in an unfounded fear complex, and has created in himself an illusion of Indian invasion.

"THE SUN" of Sri Lanka quoted him as saying during the tension-week of July, 1983, "If India decides to invade us, we will fight and may be lose, but with dignity." This message exposed his deep-rooted anxiety but this anxiety had been haunting his mind from 1982 onwards.

During an interview to "The Hindu", JRJ told, (May 1982) "Supposing she (India) invades, our principles are not in any way tarnished by India's invasion. *Take Sri Lanka and rule it. You can't rule 15 million people if they are opposed to it. If I am alive I will carry on the movement against that invasion.*"

This sort of oft-repeated utterances of JRJ whipped up the Sinhalese fury against India, as a whole, the reflection of which can be seen from the orgy of violence against all that was Indian. To them India was not only an alienation, but also a belligerant nation! What else can be the inference ?

Again when India raised mild protest, through diplomatic channels, against the passage of Public Security Ordinance (June 1983) the JRJ regime reacted very angrily and made a public issue of it. "Why didn't you raise such a voice when Srimao Bandaranaike's government promulgated similar ordinance giving the army blanket powers to bury the bodies of the killed, without inquest ?", Sri Lankan Government asked.

'SUN', the national daily of Sri Lanka asked, "*Has Indira lost her grip on India and India lost its balanced outlook in international affairs? Is her heart bleeding for the terrorists in Jaffna? Or is Tricomalee the apple of her eye?*" This is the most insinuating question, that India has ever faced !

Ironically enough, about two months back, during May, 1983, JRJ raised allegations against Srimao Bandaranaike by saying that she asked for military assistance from the US, when the Indian army marched inside Bangladesh! According to him, she expressed the fears of possible Indian invasion and now this is JRJ's turn.

This sort of fear, though unfounded, of the successive Sinhala governments often found public expressions, whipping up the fury of the Sinhala fanatics, which has culminated into the recent orgy against Indians. Their cry of wolf has seen ventilation in this cruel way !

8

IRON CURTAIN

IT is usual for the Government of Ceylon to gag the press and subject it to stiff censorship. This time the stiffness of the censor reached an unprecedental level—virtually an iron curtain was raised!

The pressmen also were put to numerous difficulties—constant checks and counter checks on all of them—frequent and wanton dislocation of telephone connections and telex services--a virtual unwritten prohibition for taking any photograph of the burning or damaged premises—the unscrupulous use of power by the censor authorities, who carried out their tasks to their whims and fancies—all made it difficult for the outside world to clearly understand the harrowing tales and estimate the colossal damage caused to the properties of Tamils. We could come across only the leaked-out reports and the tales of persons lucky to escape from the mass butchery!

PORTRAYAL OF PATRICK JONAS

Patrick Jonas, a noted Journalist, has given a vivid portrayal of how the press was gagged during the riot-torn days.

He says, "Journalists from other countries, including India, were virtually being held incommunicados. Their reports were lacerated with the blood red pencil of the censor who cut out all that she found was "objectionable". Many journalists stopped writing reports altogether since what remained after the censor went through them was a few lines. More enterprising of the scribes, however, smuggled out their reports through persons leaving the country.

"All hotels in Colombo were under orders from the Government not to allow the journalists use their telex and making a telephone call to India was an impossibility during the last week of July". *(Courtesy—The Week)*

CENSOR CAPRICIOUS

Mr. William Claiborne, Delhi-based South Asia correspondent of *Washington Post* reached Colombo on 27th July, 1983 and according to him the curfew in the island was very tight and the censorship very stiff. He stated,

"The censor was highly capricious and slashed out news without any sense of reason. Photography had been banned and one photographer had his camera smashed.

"Journalists were no longer issued curfew passes. They were given passes to go only from their hotels to the office of the censor".

Somehow he managed to get some information and reported that the *shops and restaurants of Sri Lanka nationals of Tamil origin were selectively burnt and Sinhalese shops and establishments had been left intact—even their name boards were not touched by the hooligans and looters!*

This correspondent's visit to Jaffna was completely controlled by the army. He was provided with military escort to move about in Jaffna. There was tension all round and people had closed even the windows as army men patrolled the streets.

He met the army Commander and asked him about alleged rape of Tamil women by army men, which was the cause for the ambush of 13 soldiers on July 23. But the Commander, in the characteristic style of the Sinhalese, denied it.

BBC NO EXCEPTION

Mr. Mark Tully, the BBC correspondent from Britain said that he was not allowed to report his talks with a prominent leader in Jaffna, although his party (TULF) was not banned. The censor officials virtually confiscated the news report.

PRESSMEN OF INDIA BULLIED

An Indian Press Photographer was detained by the police in Colombo on 10th August and was released only after three hours.

The films of the photographer employed by a Delhi-based fortnightly was seized and he was later told that those films would be returned if there was "nothing objectionable" in them!

Mrs. Anita Pratap of "Sunday" narrates how she was ill-treated by the army men and authorities as well. Under the caption, "To hell and back", she has given her narration thus:

"My experiences in Colombo were nightmarish. Being a woman, an Indian, an outsider, a journalist and totally alone, was quite easily the worst combination to begin with. As the riots in Sri Lanka became broad-based to encompass all Indians, any Indian was vulnerable to attack from the Sinhalese vandals on the rampage. As a journalist I was pinioned by the hawk-eyed gaze of the State authorities, particularly the censors. The Press was muzzled totally because I was an Indian correspondent.

"Getting a hotel accommodation was the first problem and for me would have remained an insurmountable one had it not been for my fortuitous meeting with Mr. Mark Tully, the BBC correspondent...

"Barely hours after I touched down in Colombo, I was kept under strict surveillance. My phone was tapped, my notes confiscated. Getting a curfew pass proved to be a Herculean task. The inspector incharge of issuing a pass refused to give me one, saying with genuine concern that if I stepped into the street during curfew it would be suicide...".

U.S. Newsman Expelled

Mr. Stewart Slavin, a journalist of United Press International (U.S.) was even expelled on 2nd August by the Sri Lanka Government for forwarding certain reports which had not been approved by the censor. He narrated his harrowing tale the next day at Bombay. He stated that he was virtually in the custody for about 12 hours on 2nd August.

Fate of Tamil Journals

The Tamil Newspapers could not resume publication even during the second week of August, 1983. Most of the journalists could not at all be seen in the open. They were either underground or cooped up in the refuge camps.

During the July riots, it is reliably learnt that the editor of the banned Tamil daily "Swathanthran" was killed in the Welikade jail massacre !

One of the houses burnt in the Sinhalese violence belonged to the editor of "Virakesari" which is owned by Mr. Wenceslaus, father-in-law of Mr. Vijay Amritharaj, Indian Tennis Star. But the 'Virakesari' building was left intact. This was not by sheer oversight—but a deliberate omission ! Sri Lanka President Mr. Jayawardene was born in this building and the Sinhalese rioters were not prepared to commit the sacrilegious act of pulling it down!

Does this not clearly indicate to the world as to who masterminded the riots? In spite of this Mrs. Jayawardene is making futile attempts to shift the burden and making a number of unconcerned persons scape-goated!

PRO-GOVERNMENT MEDIA FANNING THE FURY

Though all such systematic gagging of the press was done as regards reports reaching foreign countries, the pro-Government papers were given a free hand.

True to their masters' expectations these papers played down the enormity of the human tragedy. Their partisan reports were aimed at fanning the Sinhala fury and only a few pictures of death and destructions were carried by them! They even went to the level of taking a light-hearted approach to the carnage!

9

GLOBAL PROTESTS

SRI LANKA has seen umpteen race riots for the past 3 decades and in each and every riot, butchery, looting, arson and rape have been invariably committed by the Sinhalese.

There were, of course, the blessings of the powers-that-be for them, but this time government itself has openly come and the army, navy, air force and the police were let loose on the innocent Tamils!

This time, unlike in the past, the wave of terror and tyranny has attracted the attention of the whole world. Lovers of freedom and advocates of human rights have openly expressed their shock and concern! So far, so good ! The Tamils are lucky this time to invoke the sympathy of the whole world.

BRITAIN

The Sri Lanka Tamils, living in Britain, feared that the office of the Indian High Commission might be attacked. So, some of them maintained an all-night vigil outside the Indian High Commission in London. They lit candles and carried placards demanding India to intervene to put an end to the atrocities against Tamils in Sri Lanka. A Memorandum addressed to the Prime Minister of India, Mrs. Gandhi, was presented.

Eighty Labour Party MPs urged the British government to cancel the scheduled October (1983) visit of Sri Lanka President Mr. Jayawardene to Britain.

Mr. Edward Nellist, a Labour Member, sponsored a motion in the House of Commons, which read, "In the light of the persecution of Tamils of Sri Lanka, of the reports of mass murder, of extraction of confessions under torture and of burial of bodies without inquest following action by the security forces, we call the government to cancel the state visit of Mr. Jayawardene, scheduled for October." Of course, this motion was not passed in the parliament—but subsequently Mr. Jayawardene himself had to announce the cancellation of his visit!

In London, during the riots, the Sri Lanka Tamil community established an Information Centre to answer queries from those concerned about the welfare of their friends and relatives in the island.

NEW YORK

Members of a Marxist organisation picketed the Sri Lanka mission (28th July) to the United Nations to protest against the Sri Lankan Government's treatment of Tamils.

Members of the Sparticist League demonstrated across the street from the mission and carried placards that read, "Stop police terror against the Tamils".

SOUTH AFRICA

In Durban, South Africa, the Natal Tamil Vedic Society sent a telegram to Mr. Jayawardene urging him to take immediate action to stop the oppression against the Tamils. The society's secretary, *Mr. M.N. Pathar* said that the situation being monitored alongwith Tamil Societies in Massachussets and

New York in the US. He also said, "We are very angry and perturbed that this sort of unnecessary massacre is being perpetrated against our brothers and sisters. We want to appeal to the Indian government and especially the people of Tamil Nadu to protest against the slaughter of the Tamils."

The President of the South African Andhra Maha Sabha, *Mr. R.S. Naidoo* also condemned the violence and said that "as oppressed people ourselves, we feel for the oppressed Tamils in Sri Lanka."

AUSTRALIA

Australia's Immigration and Ethnic Affairs Minister, *Mr. Stewart West* said in a statement that he had instructed departmental officers to give top priority to sponsorship applications already lodged by Australian residents for the entry of Sri Lanka citizens affected by the disturbances.

BONN

On 24th July, 1983, about 600 Tamil refugee settlers of Sri Lanka peacefully demonstrated before the Indian embassy there and submitted a Memorandum to be forwarded to the Prime Minister of India. These refugees living in "exile" in W. Germany asked Mrs. Gandhi "to intervene in the Sri Lanka problem and rescue the Tamils from the hands of the discriminative government." Requesting the Indian government to appoint a Tamil as India's High Commissioner to Sri Lanka, the eight point memorandum also asked New Delhi to raise the problem at the U.N.

A group of Tamilians started hunger-strike also in order to focus the attention of the German people on the problem of Tamils. The police had accorded permission both for the demonstration and for the hunger-strike.

BANGLADESH

Lt. General Ershad, Chief Martial Law Administrator of

Bangladesh cancelled his scheduled state visit to Colombo. In a cable to Mr. Jayawardene, he registered his protest against the killing of Tamil Muslims in Sri Lanka and cited this as a reason for the cancellation of his trip.

WCC IN VANCOUVER (CANADA)

According to a UNI report, the Ethnic Tamils had called on the World Council of Churches, which met on 4th Aug. 1983, at Vancouver (Canada) to give high priority within the anti-racism programme to the "systematic violating of the Tamils' human rights by the government of Sri Lanka." A Tamil delegate told the sixth WCC general assembly that one million Tamils had been forced to leave their homelands since 1948.

GENEVA

The International Commission of Jurists (ICJ) in its report submitted to the U.N. Sub-Commission on Human Rights (Aug. 19, 1983), has stated that the race riots in Sri Lanka were made worse by the government indifference to the fate of Tamil minority. The ICJ also called for an independent judicial enquiry into the killing of 52 persons in jail. According to the Report, some police officers, convicted earlier for acting illegally, had been ostentatiously promoted by decision of Cabinet Ministers. The ICJ also called for the repeal of Terrorism Act, which, it said, violated the International Human Rights' Association's objectives.

UN Sub-Commission on Human Rights

UN Sub-Commission on Human Rights met at Geneva on 24th Aug. 1983. In the meeting, several human rights experts expressed concern over the ethnic violence in Sri Lanka.

Mr. Asbjorn Eide of Norway proposed the establishment of an independent commission of enquiry and said that Sri Lanka government should take steps to prevent such occurrences.

Miss Amy Young, representative of procedural aspects of International Law Institute and International Human Rights Law group, deplored in strong terms the measures taken by the Sri Lanka government in the past year leading to a "notable decline" in rule of law. She cited the enactment of Terrorism Act into a permanent law. Miss Young expressed her hope that the Sri Lanka government would make a comprehensive and objective investigation into the killings once peace had been restored.

The Sri Lanka Ambassador Mr. A.T. Jayakodi found it very hard to defend his government.

World Bank and the IMF

Mr. G.K. Reddy, the special correspondent of "The Hindu" gave the following report on Aug. 22, 1983 :

"The World Bank and IMF, which have sunk a lot of money in the last few years for salvaging Sri Lanka's stagnan economy, are reported to be cautioning the Jayawardene government against any rash political move to dislodge the Tamils from key sectors, under the guise of increased Sinhalese participation in wholesale and retail trade, take over of damaged industrial units and utilisation of public funds to repair and restore their productivity under state supervision.

"The IMF is sending a team to Colombo to survey the extent of damage done to Sri Lanka's economy by the recent violence, while reviewing the country's performance and re-assessing its foreign aid requirements *before releasing the remaining trenches of the loan commitments*."

This is the mildest way of putting things! The World Bank and IMF told the Finance Minister of Sri Lanka "in no uncertain terms that the attempts of the government to expropriate virtually the Tamil owned properties and business premises would transform Sri Lanka into another Uganda by scaring away foreign investment and depriving the country of the expertise of its own Tamil minority on purely political considerations."

This is a caution and at the same time, one cannot overlook the underlying stricture so mildly passed against the Sri Lanka government.

Loss of Reputation

The estimated loss to the property due to the arson and looting is nearly 2000 crores! It will be a great setback to the economy of Sri Lanka. But, Sri Lanka's image in the international community was more seriously affected. Overnight, Sri Lanka was put on the defensive role. Condemnation of mass killings and arson was uniform, world wide! This kind of global protests could not have been faced even by the Nazis!

10

REACTION IN INDIA

THE atrocities of the Sinhalese against the Tamils in Sri Lanka, naturally created much distress, concern and annoyance in the minds of the people of Tamil Nadu.

There were much protests, condemnations, hunger-strikes. A plethora of spontaneous processions erupted.

Lawyers, doctors, students, workers, Government servants and all classes of citizens without exception registered their protests and condemnations against the orgy,—the mode of their expression varied, but the mood was the same !

The people of Tamil Nadu, in short, looked raged and dismayed, panic-stricken, frenzied and one could see from their expressions that their blood boiled.

Thousands of telegrams were sent to the Prime Minister of India, urging to take speedy and necessary steps to save the Tamils.

SHIP-IMMOLATION BIDS

As many as 20 self-immolation bids were reported in all over Tamil Nadu. The Honourable Chief Minister Mr. M.G. Ramachandran had to give a frantic call through AIR, requesting the revolutionary youth, to desist from any act of self-immolation.

RELIGIOUS HEADS

Jagathguru Sankarachariar, Kunrakudi Adigalar, Adeenam of Madurai and such religious heads condemned the violence perpetrated against the Tamils.

All Christian institutions registered their protests—many of them conducted protest rallies also in places like Madras, Trichy, Madurai and Coimbatore.

The religious heads of Muslims also condemned the orgy of violence. In Trichy, some Moulvis and Christian fathers went on a token hunger-strike under the leadership of Kunrakudi Adigalar, a reputed Tamil scholar and religious head of Hindus.

POLITICAL REACTION

The political parties in Tamil Nadu vied with one another in focussing and championing the cause of Tamils in Sri Lanka.

The Chief Minister, Mr. M.G. Ramachandran announced a week long State-mourning condemning the violence in Ceylon. All political leaders were summoned and it was unanimously decided to conduct a State-wide Bandh on Aug. 2, 1983. Accordingly the people of Tamil Nadu expressed their feelings in unmistakable terms—the response was splendid—the bandh was total, peaceful! In this Bandh, it is worth mentioning that the Central Government also played its own significant role by announcing holiday to all the Central Government offices and concerns. No train movement, air-service! It seemed everything in Tamil Nadu came to a halt that day, by a magic wand of the Almighty! The Govt. of Tamil Nadu decided to simplify the Independence Day function dispensing with rallies and such ostentations!

The all party delegation, headed by Mr. M.G. Ramchandran, Chief Minister of Tamil Nadu, met the Prime Minister Mrs. Indira Gandhi and submitted a Memorandum requesting her to take suitable and immediate measures and also to take up the matter to the International Forums and seek redressal.

The ruling AIADMK issued a clarion call to all the members of the party to wear black shirts from 16th August, upto 14th September, 1983.

DMK

The DMK, in its District Conference (30 and 31st July, 1983) condemned the violence in strongest of words possible. The DMK decided to conduct 'Stop Train' (Rail Roko) agitation on 4th August, in order to draw the attention of the Centre to take effective steps in this regard. The Central Government announced that there would be no train service on that day, in its bid to avoid any violence or untoward incident that might arise in the wake of an agitation. It is said that the Chief Minister of Tamil Nadu requested Mrs. Gandhi to do so and his request was heeded to.

Mr. Karunanidhi, President of the DMK and Mr. Anbazhagan, General Secretary of the party, resigned their memberships in the Legislative Assembly of Tamil Nadu. This was to express their deep sympathy to the Tamils of Sri Lanka and to condemn the Central Government for not taking effective steps to prevent the orgy of violence. The DMK also conducted State-wide meetings and in those meetings, copies of Anti-Secessionist Bill of Sri Lanka were burnt, as a mark of protest against this Bill.

SACRIFICE MARCH

Mr. Nedumaran, leader of the Kamaraj Congress led a march with thousands of volunteers from Madurai. It was termed by him as a "Sacrifice March" and he announced that he, along with his followers, will cross the Palk Strait through country boats and reach Talai Mannar, without any arms in their hands. This sacrifice march, according to Mr. Nedumaran, was intended to express to the world the deep feelings of emotion and anguish of Tamils and also intended to 'goad' the Centre to take speedy measures to save the lives of Tamils.

Mr. Kumari Anandan, leader of Gandhi Kamaraj National Congress announced the burning of the effigies of Mrs. Gandhi—but he could not do so, since he was arrested prior hand. He then proceeded to Rameswaram and joined the sacrifice march of Mr. Nedumaran.

FORMATION OF TULF BRANCH AT MADRAS

Mr. T.R. Janardhanan, M.L.C. Chief Whip, resigned his whip post in the Legislative Council, so that he could devote his full attention to the cause of Tamils in Sri Lanka. This was hailed by one and all as a very bold and prudent step. He also formed a branch of the TULF at Madras, and this branch was later approved by Mr. Amirthalingam, Secretary General, during his visit to Madras.

A.P. ASSEMBLY

Andhra Pradesh Legislative Assembly unanimously passed a resolution condemning the violence perpetrated against Tamils in Sri Lanka. The Chief Ministers of Karnataka and Kerala also condemned the violence.

INDIAN PARLIAMENT

The Indian Parliament was very much perturbed and almost in a frenzied mood. The condemnation in the Parliament against the violence was unanimous. The speakers went to the extent of asking the Government of India immediately to send its armed forces to protect the Tamils. Some wanted that the matter should be referred immediately to the UN requesting it to send its Security forces to safeguard the Tamils in Sri Lanka. Though all the political parties condemned the violence, the DMK and the AIADMK were most vociferous.

New Delhi also witnessed a number of agitations as a result of the violence in Sri Lanka. The Cong. (I) MPs of Tamil Nadu, under the leadership of Mr. G. Karupiah Moopanar, picketed before the Sri Lanka High Commission Office. Mr. L. Ganesan M.P. and Gopalswamy M.P. both belonging to the D.M.K. went on hunger-strike at Delhi and they concluded their strike only after three days at the request of Mr. Karunanidhi, leader of the DMK. Almost all the MPs of Tamil Nadu were wearing either black shirts or black batches during the whole of July-August session of Parliament as a mark of their mourning for the violence in Sri Lanka.

Mr. S. Ramachandran, then Minister for Electricity (now Food Minister—Dec. 1986) in his address in a Sub-Committee of the United Nations condemned the violence perpetrated against the Tamils by the government of Sri Lanka. He elaborately explained as to how it was not purely an internal matter because of the repurcussions on the Indian economy, due to wave of immigrations.

So, this time (July-August, 1983) much awakening could be seen throughout the country, much in contrast to the awakening during waves of violence on previous occasions. The anti-India overtone of Sri Lanka Government also helped to a great extent to hammer unity, to arouse a consensus of opinion and to awaken the feelings of all people in India. Miss Jayalalitha, Mr. L. Ganesan, Mr. Gopalswamy all these members of Rajya Sabha, in their speeches, condemned the Sri Lankan government for unleashing inhuman violence against the Tamils.

Mr. S.D. Somasundaram, the then Minister for Revenue Govt. of Tamil Nadu, wrote a number of articles in his weekly "PORVAL", giving a historical survey of the plight of Tamils in Sri Lanka, quoting profusely from the speeches and writings of Anna.

Mr. Kalimuthu, the then Minister for Agriculture in the government of Tamil Nadu was very vociferous in condemning the Jayawardane regime.

TESO (Tamil Eelam Supporters' Organisation) was formed under the leadership of Mr. Karunanidhi, leader of the D.M.K.

It conducted a number of conferences in Tamil Nadu focussing the plight of the Tamils in Sri Lanka.

POST-INDIRA PERIOD—SOME HALLMARKS

Mr. Rajiv Gandhi, Prime Minister of India, showed a sort of soft pedalling in this issue in the beginning. But, later on he exerted maximum pressure on the Sri Lankan government to come round for talks.

Mr. G. Parthasarathy paved the way for talks even when Mrs. Indira Gandhi was alive. His efforts would ever be remembered by Tamils all over the world.

Round Table conference was arranged at Thimpu, Nepal, due to the efforts of Indian Prime Minister Mr. Rajiv Gandhi.

High level talks between Mr. Rajiv Gandhi and Mr. Jayawardene were held at Bangalore on 16th and 17th Nov. 1986, when the session of the SAARC (South Asian Association for Regional Co-operation) was held there.

Mr. Prabhakaran of LTTE was taken to Bangalore by the Chief Minister of Tamil Nadu, Mr. M.G. Ramachandran. Mr. S. Ramachandran, known as Panruti Ramachandran, Food Minister of Tamil Nadu played an active role in the mediation. His clarity of thought has been very much useful in this regard.

Mr. P. Chidambaram, Minister for State for Home Affairs, government of Tamil Nadu also played a very vital role in solving the ethnic problem of Sri Lanka. He paid numerous visits to Sri Lanka, had a number of talks with the various groups of Tamil leaders and by his soft nature and clear understanding is rendering invaluable service to the cause of the Sri Lankan Tamils.

Meanwhile some reports are coming about the struggle between the various groups of Liberation forces. It is heartrending and the Indian public feels that these groups are falling prey to the sinister moves of the Sri Lankan government.

11

A WORD ABOUT JRJ

MR. JAYAWARDENE'S tenure of office has been extended and he has to be in power, provided everything goes on smoothly, as scheduled. The Tamils of Sri Lanka have to be under his rule for some more years—and so his calibre as well as his character is very relevant to predict the future of the Tamils there!

RACE AFFINITY

Mr. Junius Richard Jayawardene or JRJ as he is often called, exposed his true colour when he was interviewed by the Indian pressmen on Aug. 17, 1983. When told that one of the Indian correspondent, interviewing him was a Bengali, he greeted that correspondent, saying that Bengalis and the Sinhalese belong to one race and hail from one and the same place. He openly said that they belonged to the 'Aryan race' as opposed to the 'Dravidian race' to which the Tamils belong !

The supremacy of Aryan race was almost eulogised by Herr Hitler and JRJ has slowly stepped into his shoes !

Not only that! This is his calculated attempt to drive a wedge between the Tamils and other linguistic groups in India.

JRJ expressed his avowed anti-Tamil feelings even during 1944. During the discussion to the Constituent Assembly JRJ spearheaded a motion making Sinhala language a compulsory one in the curriculum in all the Schools in Sri Lanka.

The notorious Citizenship Act of 1948, depriving the civil rights of 10 million Tamils working in plantations was actually sponsored by JRJ.

When Banda-Chelvanayagam Pact was signed, JRJ condemned the pact very violently and led the notorious "Kandi voyage" and with the help of the Buddhist priests and Sinhala fanatics, he laid the foundation for the 'abrogation' of that pact. Mr. Bandaranaike was actually pressurised to succumb! During that March, JRJ fomented fire and fury in the official daily of UNP.

Here are his words:

"*Sinhalese youth, awake, arise! Do not allow the Tamils to rule our country. In the interest of the country kill as many Tamils as you can! If you cannot, better end yourselves. Let us march, march to our goal!*"

Yes, these are the very words of the Dharmishta of Sri Lanka. What can the Tamils expect of this butcher, except savage attacks?

During the Presidential election of 1982, the same JRJ gave sweet assurances to Tamils when he addressed a meeting in Jaffna! "Saving the lives of Mr. Kuttimani and Mr. Jegan is my foremost objective", he declared.

But after ascending the gadi, he changed his tone. When the TULF nominated Mr. Kuttimani as an MP, JRJ vociferously declared "I will never allow this, till I breathe my last!"

Does this not clearly show how callous and cunning JRJ is? It is not a clear testimony of his deceit and treachery? It is also said that he inherited these innate and inhuman qualities from his forefathers. "SUNDAY" writes,

"J.R. Jayawardene's great grand-father had played an ignoble and treacherous role in the history of the island. He guided the first British contingent to the court of the Kandyian King and thereby laid the foundation for the dissolution of the Kandyian Kingdom. Jayawardene's strange fascination for the British Royalty stems from this mean act of his forefather".

A traditional treacherer as he is, the Tamils have to carry on conciliatory talks with him—No other go!

JRJ, a fragile old man, has been volatile in nature—vociferous always against the Tamils. He is vile-minded, venom-tongued, villainy-eyed and vulture-nosed always too ready to pounce upon the Tamils and suck their blood. In arrogance he is an equal to Herr Hitler, in cold-bloodedness he is comparable to the Czars of Russia, in demogogy and deceipt he is capable of excelling even Goebels. He is diabolically cunning like proverbial jackals combined with the cruelty of blood-thirsty panthers! He is a demogogic, double-tongued, unscrupulous and blood-thirsty politician. In short, he is the hardest nut to crack!

12

WHAT IS THE WAY OUT ?

1. Political serfdom and subjection.

2. Denial of equal status to Tamil language.

3. Denial of equal opportunities for the Tamils in the sphere of education and employment.

4. State-sponsored colonisations in Tamil-dominated areas.

5. Irrepairable loss sustained by the Tamils, their economic position having been completely shattered.

6. Buddhist supremacy and predominance over all other religions, because of its having been acclaimed as the national religion.

7. The superiority complex of the Sinhalese and their frequent acts of vandalism, massacre and the like.

8. The adamance and arrogance of the Sinhalese leaders, never heeding to the just demands of the Tamils.

The Tamils have to seek a permanent solution to all the

problems listed above. First, they should get a sense of security and then only other things can follow.

In the light of the utterances of JRJ almost justifying the carnage, Tamils cannot be expected to acquire any sense of security.

TALES AND TALKS

At the instance of the Indian Government through its envoy Mr. G. Parthasarathy, an attempt was made to bring about the Sinhalese leaders and the Tamil leaders to the Conference table. It is the wish of all the well meaning people that the talks should materialise and something good must emerge !

If in the talks, mere assurances are given by the Sinhalese leaders, they will be of no use because the Tamils have seen so many of their assurances ! The Tamils also have seen that none of their assurances were kept up, promises fulfilled ! so, no use getting mere assurances.

When a special correspondent of "The Hindu" met some of the TULF leaders in Jaffna (during the second week of August, 1983) they said that all their earlier talks with the Sinhalese leaders were futile because "they never meant a word of what they said." The correspondent sums up his interview as follows :

"Thus in 1957 Bandaranaike-Chelvanayagam pact was signed, only to be abrogated soon; then there was the 1965 Dudley Senanayaka-Chelvanayagam agreement, which was not given effect to at all; and rounds of discussion with SLFP leaders were between 1972 and 1976 and with the UNP leaders between 1977 and 1983 failed to produce any worthwhile result". (The Hindu—Aug. 18, 1983).

Mr. Amirthalingam, who was then in Madras, told, "My experience has been that the Sri Lanka Government had agreed to do a number of things during the negotiations, but they were never implemented. It is this record of going back on solemn assurances which made the Tamil community to lose its confidence in the Government."

Therefore the Tamils will no more be cheated by mere assurances—there should be something concrete, so as to allay their fears and ameliorate their conditions.

OUR-DATED PROPOSALS

Mr. H.W. Jayawardene, brother of JRJ, during his visit to Delhi sounded some proposals to Mrs. Gandhi. The proposals were like full implementation of the laws relating to the District Development Councils, the use of Tamil as provided for as a national language in the present constitution, repeal of Prevention of Terrorism Act. But Mrs. Gandhi clearly expressed her view to him *(on 12th Aug. 1983), that those out-dated proposals would not meet the aspirations of the Tamils, especially after the recent tragic events.* So, in a very subtle way Mrs. Gandhi has expressed the sentiments of the Tamils.

ENTHRONE TAMIL FIRST

Bishop Deogu Pillai, the Bishop of Jaffna, in his interview to "The Hindu" stated that there was a stubborn resistance among the Sinhalese to making Tamil also an official language. But the Tamils would not be satisfied unless their language is given the status of an official language in parity with Sinhalese. "That must come first ! Not a mere 'national language', which means nothing", he said. But there is stubborn resistance for that and the person in gadi is JRJ, with an unmistakable record of avowed bitterness against Tamil. We cannot expect much conciliatory measures from him, a person who is reluctant to give even a lip sympathy to the affected Tamils in the recent orgy of violence !

DECLARATION OF WAR

Bishop Deogu Pillai of Jaffna has also stated, "The additional powers given to the armed forces in the North and North East (through Prevention of Terrorism Act) is tantamount to a declaration of war against the Tamil minority community".

It is a misnomer to call the recent violences in Sri Lanka as mere riots—it is a genocide, an open undeclared war against the Tamils, Indians. The Government which has got the bounden duty to safeguard the rights, liberties, lives and properties of persons not only failed to do so but actively co-operated with the lynch mobs.

On numerous occasions, the Government vehicles were used to carry the goondas and also the looted goods.

Trains stopped at the whims and fancies of the frenzied Sinhalese mob, so as to facilitate their acts of vandalism.

Police, Navy and Air force personnel, all these so called 'Security Machineries' actively participated in the acts of violence, butchery, looting, arson and rape and what not !

Ministers like Cyril Mathew openly came to the streets and instigated the Sinhalese mob.

What more evidence is required to show that the JRJ regime itself is up against the Tamils and it has conducted a pitched battle against them.

Under such circumstances, whatever be the talks between the Sinhalese and the Tamil leaders, the Tamil minority would not feel satisfied unless they sever all connections with the Sinhalese—So, nothing short of sovereign Eelam State can satisfy them, can fulfil their aspirations. The Tamils have been so ruthlessly driven to that extent.

A bachelor, who reached Madras on 11th Aug. 1983, after having undergone a virtual confinement, told, "People like me who are Sinhala citizens and whose families have been living in that country for generations, never subscribed to the Eelam movement until the Sinhalese conspiracy to annihilate the Tamil race was exposed and the confidence in the Jayawardene Government was shattered".

Mr. Uma Maheshwaran, Chairman of the Peoples Liberation Organisation for Tamil Eelam (PLOT) has stated that this movement was only the result of the failure of the all democratic means to restore their just rights to Tamils.

In a letter addressed to Mr. Premadasa, Prime Minister of Sri Lanka, Mr. Prabhakaran, Chairman of the Liberation Tigers of Tamil Eelam (LTTE) stated, "the guerilla warfare, the form of the popular struggle we are committed to, is not borne out of blind militancy or adventurism, but arose out of historical necessity; out of concrete conditions of intolerable national oppression."

So, various organisations have sprung up, out of historical necessity and all of them demand in one voice, the Sovereign Eelam State.

Oh, Separation—is it not a sacrilege? Is it not a heinous cry ?—the Sinhalese leaders ask, of course, donning themselves on 'national' garb, but camouflaging their heinous intentions! Here is the answer, in the words of *Mr. Francis Wheen.* He has written in "The Times," London thus:

"*If one remains unconvinced (by the argument for Eelam), the Tamils produce their Clincher 'What is the alternative?'*

"*It is difficult to think of one. Ever since Ceylon became independent in 1948, the Tamils* have been a persecuted minority.

"Mr. Vijay Kumaratunga, the leader of a leftist party SLMP, is not able to speak freely on his own party platform. Bombs are hurled at him. This shows that no Sinhalese party expressing support to the Tamils in any way can flourish there. This is why we say circumstances do not permit us the luxury of trusting the Sinhalese politicians".

—Mr. V. Prabhakaran, the LTTE leader
in his interview to "THE HINDU"
(5-9-1986)

Their language and culture have been downgraded; they *have been discriminated against in employment and education; and they have been subjected to violent physical attack. Genocide is a word that must be used with care; but how else is one to describe the impulse which guided the Sinhalese lynch-mobs this week? (last week of July, 1983). Alarming members of Sinhalese now wish to see that the Tamils driven off the face of Sri Lanka."*

The chase between the two races has widened too much—no amount of conciliatory moves or measures can bridge the gulf better to part away !

Panther and goat cannot co-exist—reptiles and frogs cannot live together—beasts are always beasts and pet animals cannot be left to be tended by them !

Therefore, the Tamils living in Sri Lanka have got no other alternative but to form a separate Eelam State—that alone will be a permanent solution for the Tamils. Talking about the unity of Sri Lanka is nothing but an attempt to make Tamils live in the abode of poisonous reptiles and scorpions.

Mr. Amirthalingam, very crisply pointed this out at *Delhi when he said, "We can even separate by mutual consent as did Malaysia and Singapore. It will be a divorce by agreement"*.

Why not the salient examples of Canada and Cyprus be followed? Let us hope and hope that sagacity and statesmanship would prevail, not sullenness or short-sightedness!

INDEX